MW01233274

LOVE YOURSELF FIRST

DO YOUR INTROSPECTION TO UNBOX YOUR LIFE AND LOOK AHEAD FREEDOM FROM FEAR

By

Eldon Wells

Important

The book is not intended to provide medical advice or to take the place of any treatment of your personal physician. Readers are advised to consult their own doctors or other qualified health professional regarding the treatment of medical conditions. The author shall not be held liable or responsible for any misunderstanding or misuse of the information contained in this book. The information is not indeed to diagnose, treat or cure any disease.

It's important to remember that the author of this book is not a doctor/therapist/medical professional. only opinions based upon his own personal experiences or research are cited. The author does not offer medical advice or prescribe any treatments. For any health or medical issues – you should be talking to your doctor first.

Table of Contents

INTRODUCTION _____ 5

CHAPTER 1 _____ 9
  UNBOX YOUR LIFE _____ 9
    *What Does "Unbox your life" Means?*_____ 10
    How Positive Affirmations Can Change Your Life _____ 21
CHAPTER 2 _____ 25
  DO YOUR INTROSPECTION _____ 25
    *Focus the Mind of the Positive*_____ 26
    *The Sky is Your Limit*_____ 29
    How to Develop Your Creative Side _____ 32
    Listen to Your Inner Thought _____ 38
    Mental images Work _____ 40
    Taking Care of Your Mental Health _____ 43
CHAPTER 3 _____ 47
  DAILY HABIT MAKEOVER _____ 47
    Dispelling fears for a more positive outlook _____ 48
    Overcoming dissociation _____ 50
    Overcoming the doubt _____ 52
    Overcoming feelings of helplessness _____ 54
    Overcoming internal conflicts _____ 57
    Overcoming Bullying _____ 59
    *Overcoming the need to be in control*_____ 62
    *Overcoming the trauma*_____ 64
CHAPTER 4 _____ 69
  FREEDOM FORGE _____ 69
    *Developing Your Self-Image*_____ 70
    Change the shape of your personal image _____ 72
    How keeping a journal can help you succeed _____ 74
    *Stop underestimating your value*_____ 79
    Developing your full potential _____ 82
    Increase your self-esteem by running _____ 85
    *How to unearth your hidden forces*_____ 87
    How NLP can help you _____ 90

CONCLUSION _____ 97

  ABOUT THE AUTHOR ELDON WELLS _____ 99

INTRODUCTION

People move through ideals and goals and monitor their path towards them, continuously comparing their perception of their behaviour against the reference standards. When the individual perceives a discrepancy between their current state and the goal, they seek behavioural strategies to reduce this discrepancy.

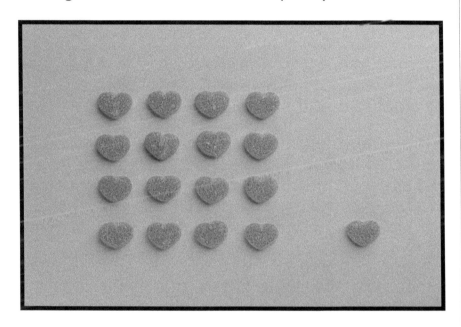

Some of these ideal plans are linked to concrete habits, for example, the idea of going to the gym twice a week. Others are linked to more abstract ideals to be achieved, such as becoming a sporty and dynamic person.

In general, the perception of a distance between how we are and how we would like to generate negative emotions of sadness so that we are led in some way to minimise this perceived difference.

There are, however, two types of ideals that have studied: models in the strict sense of the word, i.e. experiences, concepts and reference standards to strive for and refer to, and opposing ideals, i.e. situations, real or symbolic people, goals and circumstances from which people try to distance themselves and keep away because they judge them negatively.

Common sense and literature assume a negative role of ideals on self-esteem, especially if they are too ambitious and unattainable.

In general, despite the clear value that self-regulation towards goals has for society, as it pushes the individual to improve and strive towards new plans, the pursuit of ideals has an individual cost in terms of mental resources and a sense of one's worth.

Sometimes, the self-analysis that helps define a person's self-esteem has cognitive distortions, i.e. thoughts that affect one's self-regard.

Several cognitive distortions are:

Cognitive inferences, through which individuals accrue arbitrary ideas about themselves without the backing of absolute, objective data;

Selective abstractions extrapolated, through which a small negative detail becoming symbolic and representative of one's way of being;

Over-generalisations, whereby one led to generalise starting, for example, from a single personality trait that distinguishes an individual or from a single experiential episode that has seen him/her as a protagonist;

Maximisation, which allows one to implement the harmful effects of a single action carried out;

Minimisation, which allows one to reduce the positive impact of some event;

Personalisation, which helps one to feel guilty for some adverse event that has occurred;

Dichotomous thinking, which does not allow for nuances in the assumption of responsibility, leading the analysis back to the constructs of everything and nothing (black and white vision).

Self-esteem and causal attributions

The process by which individuals evaluate themselves is also due to causal attributions. Put in simpler terms, and people often try to explain an event by linking it to a cause. Usually, there is a tendency to attribute an achieved success to an external cause, such as luck, or an internal cause, such as tenacity.

You may have noticed that many people are considered beautiful by society but who feel inadequate and are always looking for something missing to feel comfortable in their bodies finally.

At the same time, despite having minor defects, some people love themselves, live their bodies with serenity, and convey this serenity to the outside world in terms of self-confidence.

It is essential to help people who do not accept themselves and exaggerate their faults because they think they cannot lead a rewarding life. Instead, they need to become aware of the erroneous beliefs that underlie their self-perception and then subject these false beliefs to critical examination to regain a positive image of themselves.

We must keep in mind that the mind is 'like a lens: the vision of oneself and one's body is through this lens which can modify, deform, enlarge or distort what it observes'.

Therefore, we must learn about this lens and its filters because it affects not only the way we see our bodies but the way we see ourselves in general. In turn, the way we see ourselves is the foundation of the way we see our environment, our life.

That is why we have to neutralise the distorted views that do not allow us to love ourselves as we are: give your swan a chance and never let anyone convince you that you are just an ugly duckling and that nothing can change you.

Chapter 1

UNBOX YOUR LIFE

WHAT DOES "UNBOX YOUR LIFE" MEANS?

Our prospective and attitude on life in general plays a very important role in how happy we are in life and how successful we become. Someone who thinks positively about everything will be more relaxed, calm and smiling than someone who is always looking on the wrong side, letting stress get to him or her and constantly frowning.

Not only does the way you think and feel affect you, it also affects those around you, in short, our mood affects our day. Developing and maintaining a positive outlook is essential if you want to lead a positive and fulfilling life.

There are many ways to develop a more positive perspective and begin to change the way you think and feel about many situations you encounter on a daily basis.

Changing your attitude and not falling back into negative thinking will take time, but in time the new perspective will become second nature.

The five main key points to remember when changing your perspective are:

1. Turn your thinking into positive thinking and practice positive thinking daily. You should put your mind to completing one task at a time and think only of a positive outcome and how good you will feel when you have completed the task. Never give in to doubt and let yourself believe that you have taken on too much and move on.

---

2. Don't let your conversations become negative, when in a conversation it is easy to let others discourage you, especially if they have a negative view of life. Don't be tempted to go back to your old ways, turn negative conversations into positive ones and look for the good in everything and every situation.

3. Look for the positive in those around you and point it out, so you can encourage a positive attitude around you.

4. Whatever you are doing in your daily life, always look for the good in it, even though it may be a boring task that you normally hate to do and that leaves you feeling negative, try to find something in it that makes it a more positive situation.

5. Never allow yourself to be distracted or fooled into returning to negativity, it takes time to change the way you feel and think and if you have been depressed with yourself and the world for a long time, then your new point of view will take some time to register and stay.

Over time, you will discover that many areas of your life can be changed simply by changing your perspective from a negative to a more positive one. You will discover that your self-esteem improves, you become more popular, you feel happier and more confident than before, you are able to face the tasks you used to hate without causing stress and anxiety and your relationships improve. These are just some of the areas where you can improve and gain a more positive perspective and therefore lead a more positive life.

Do you have a Self-esteem?

Realizing your Self-esteem has nothing to do with checking your bank balance, it's about you, the person you are in life. We give others respect, love and consideration, but how often do we give ourselves our due? The way you value yourself is based on the self-esteem you have, your self-esteem shows you how much you really value yourself. A healthy self-esteem leads to independence, happiness, and flexibility, the ability to adapt easily to changes, cooperation and a positive view of any situation. Low or unhealthy self-esteem, on the contrary, only leads to irrational thoughts, unhappiness, fear of the new, rigidity, defensiveness and a negative view of life in general.

The way we see ourselves has a lot to do with the way others see us, if we are happy, smiling and full of confidence then others see us as someone they want to be close to, if we respect ourselves and portray ourselves then others will respect you too, after all how can you ask for respect from others if you don't even respect yourself? So finding and developing your self-esteem is all about developing your self-esteem, so let's take a look at esteem.

High Self-Esteem

If you have high Self-esteem you will see certain traits in yourself and how you see yourself, the traits related to high self-esteem or self-worth are

- You are confident in your abilities

- You allow yourself to show your true feelings to others

- You don't have intimacy problems in relationships

- You are able to recognize and take pride in your accomplishments in life

- It is easy to forgive yourself for your mistakes and also to forgive others.

Low Self-Esteem

Similarly, if you have self-esteem problems or low self-esteem, then you will follow a certain pattern in your thoughts and ways, if you have low self-esteem problems, then you will see the following points in yourself

- You don't believe in yourself and are very insecure

- You have trouble showing and accepting intimacy in relationships

- You never let your true feelings show

- You never recognize and give yourself credit for your achievements

- You have an inability to forgive yourself or other

- You resist change at every opportunity

Developing Your Self-esteem

There are many ways to increase self-esteem and change to a more positive and healthy perspective of yourself, here are some tips to develop and increase your self-esteem.

- Don't take other people's criticism seriously, listen to what they say and learn from it.

- Take some time for yourself every day, meditate, look inside yourself and realize all your good points and imagine that you can change the bad ones for more positive ones.

- Celebrate and take pride in the smallest achievements you make.

- Do something you like to do every day, like take a walk in the sun or take a bubble bath.

- Never deprive yourself of something you enjoy, if you know you shouldn't do it, do it anyway and stop scolding yourself about it.

- Speak positively to yourself, repeat the affirmations to chase away all negative thoughts and feelings.

The benefit of using positive self-discussion

One of greatest influences we can use to our advantage in life is ourselves. In particular, we can use our thoughts because they influence our feelings and therefore can have a profound effect

---

on the way we face life in general. By learning to control our self-talk and turning it into positive rather than negative self-talk, which most people do unconsciously throughout the day, you can begin to gain more control over every aspect of your life and make essential changes.

Your ability to succeed in life depends largely on how you approach life. A positive mental attitude leads to a confident and ultimately more successful person than a person filled with negativity, leading to a lack of self-confidence and low self-esteem. By adopting a positive attitude, one sees life in a different way from that of negativity; a positive attitude leads to seeing the good in people and in the world, which leads to optimism and success. Your quality of life is based on how you think and feel in each moment and changing the way you think can dramatically change how you see life and how you deal with it.

The person who goes through life with optimism and a positive attitude is better able to face life and the problems it sometimes presents, is able to recover from life's problems or setbacks. The optimistic person will see the problem for what it is, nothing more than a temporary setback that he or she can overcome and move forward. When he or she looks at life in this optimistic way, the person is able to take full control over his or her thoughts and feelings and turn a negative situation into a more positive one simply by altering the way he or she thinks. Since thoughts can be positive or negative and you can only have one thought in mind at any given time, choosing the positive will keep your thoughts, feelings and actions optimistic, leading to a happier person who is able to achieve their goals much more easily.

Use positive self-control in your daily life

- You should use positive self-control throughout the day in order to establish a new thought pattern, you have probably established a negative thought pattern for many years and this will take time to overcome, to begin with you should try to repeat the positive self-control about 50 times during the day, this can be achieved by repeating positive statements quietly to yourself or out loud. Positive dialogue can be used for many different aspects of your life, it can help you overcome difficult situations, gain more confidence in yourself, help you stop habits, recover more quickly from an illness or make changes in your life in general. Popular phrases or sentences that can be used in positive self-talk include

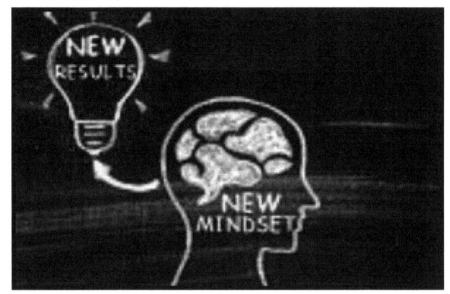

- I have an interesting challenge ahead of me - this could be used when there is a problem in life or there is some difficulty, instead of looking at the situation in a negative way and thinking that I have a problem, thinking that it is a challenge is a much more positive way of dealing with it.

- I like the person I am - this could be used to reinforce self-confidence and gain respect for oneself and the person one is, similar statements could be "I am the best", "I am a good person" or "I have many excellent qualities".

- I know I can do this - this could be used if you are faced with a certain task that you previously doubted your ability to conquer, in the same way you could say "I have the ability to conquer this" or "this is not a problem for me".

- I am full of health, energy and vitality - this can be used to foster good feelings about your health either after you have been ill or while you are recovering from an illness.

- I feel fulfilled as a person - this can be used to encourage good overall positive thoughts about yourself and the world you live in.

HOW POSITIVE AFFIRMATIONS CAN CHANGE YOUR LIFE

Having positive attitude is the key to being happy and leading a successful life, our thoughts play a very important role in how we feel and positive thinking leads to a confident and happy person in life, while negativity leads to low self-esteem and missing out on many things in life. Often we talk to ourselves about things without realizing that we are doing it, every day hundreds of negative thoughts wander freely through our minds, we lower ourselves too much and sow the seeds of doubt. There is a simple little tool that you can use throughout the day to help change these negative thoughts and instill a more positive way of thinking; the use of daily positive affirmations can dramatically change your life for the better. They can make you more confident, more aware, more self-assured and change your life in many more ways for the better.

What are Positive affirmations?

POSITIVE AFFIRMATIONS can be used during the day anywhere and anytime you need them, the more you use them, the more easily the positive thoughts will take over from the negative ones and you will see the benefits in your life. An affirmation is a simple technique that is used to change the negative complacency that we are rarely aware of, to look at your life with a more positive attitude. Most of us have been bombarded with negative thoughts for many years, so changing your thoughts and your way of thinking won't happen overnight, but if you hold onto the affirmations, they will work once you have retrained your way of thinking. There are many different affirmation techniques for dealing with different situations in life and the most popular and successful ones are listed below.

The Mirror Technique

THIS TECHNIQUE HELPS you to appreciate yourself and to develop awareness and self-esteem. You should stand in front of a mirror, preferably a full-body one, either only in your underwear or better still naked. Start at the head and work your way down the body saying out loud what you like about the areas of your body, for example you could say "I like the way my hair shines, the little color differences where the light gives it" or "my eyes are a lovely shade of They shine and sparkle; my eyes are a wonderful feature" take your time and slowly go through your whole body building a more positive image of yourself.

The "Anywhere" Technique...

THIS TECHNIQUE CAN be used anywhere and whenever you are caught thinking a negative thought, when you realize you are having a negative thought think about turning down a volume button inside your head so that you turn it down enough not to hear it anymore. Then think of a positive affirmation to replace the negative one and turn the volume up again by repeating it to yourself.

The Landfill Technique

IF YOU HAVE NEGATIVE thoughts write them on a piece of paper, roll the paper into a ball and throw it in the trash can, by doing this you are telling yourself that these thoughts are nothing but trash and that's where they belong.

The Meditation Technique

Find a quiet place where you can relax for 5 or 10 minutes, close your eyes and let your environment empty itself of all thoughts and feelings. Start repeating your affirmation to yourself over and over again while you focus on the words you are repeating and believe in what you are saying.

Chapter 2

DO YOUR INTROSPECTION

FOCUS THE MIND OF THE POSITIVE

We all go Through Difficult times in life, that's life; it can't always be a bed of roses. However, life is what you do, and by staying positive in the bad times as well as the good, you can make all the difference and get through the hard times with a smile.

But the big question is: "How do you stay positive when things get tough?" Staying optimistic at times like this is the last thing you think about, but it should be the first thing you do, you need to think positively now more than ever. The key to staying positive is to take your mind off your problems and worries and revitalize it. This is especially true when you are having a bad day and feel sorry for yourself and want to sit down and cry. Here are some excellent tips for maintaining a positive attitude in life, no matter what is going on around you.

• If you find yourself around those who are negative, then get rid of them, negativity has a way of passing from person to person and they will drag you down with them.

• Don't sit in front of the TV for hours, the news is depressing, the police stores feature violence and death, and negativity in some form is found in almost every program. If you watch television, watch a more positive program such as a nature documentary that shows the wonderful world in all its glory or a comedy.

- Spend as much time as you can with your family and loved ones, do something together that everyone enjoys and aim to have a family night at least once a week where you can spend quality time together.

- At times when you feel particularly low and negativity begins to creep in, listen to a motivational CD or repeat positive affirmations to yourself to bring back a positive attitude.

- Take time each day to do something you enjoy that doesn't require you to make decisions, something that relaxes you to the maximum.

- Try to do something you wouldn't normally do, something you don't like and that is out of character, take up a new hobby or sport you would never have dreamed of doing.

- Do some exercise, it can be something like just taking a walk outside and it's totally free or go to the gym or participate in activities like yoga.

- Set goals for yourself to get ahead and when you do, give yourself a little reward for doing so.

- Learn techniques that will allow you to draw attention to yourself and quickly focus on the task at hand.

- Use affirmations throughout the day to instill self-confidence and positive thoughts and feelings

- Always look for the best in bad situations, although things may not be what we expect if you look hard enough you may find that they are not as bad as they seem.

- Remember that the situation will not last forever, this is just a temporary stage you are going through and it will get better.

THE SKY IS YOUR LIMIT

You can achieve anything you set your mind to, the sky is really your limit, and as long as you follow a few simple steps, you are able to achieve anything in life. The key to success is, to be absolutely committed to achieving what you want, to take the necessary steps to achieve what you want and change your focus and stick to this new approach until you achieve what you want. The steps are relatively easy to follow and changes can easily be made to determine your success in whatever you want to achieve in life, let's take a closer look at the steps above.

Commitment

You must take positive and decide exactly what you want to achieve in life and set your goal, once you have set your mind to what you want you must go into it with total conviction and commitment. When you plan and set your goal you must have the firm conviction that you will achieve your goal no matter what it takes, you must visualize your goal from beginning to end and see yourself achieving whatever you set out to do.

Take the Necessary Steps

Once you have decided to go for it and committed yourself, the next step is to start acting to achieve your goal. Taking the first step is actually the hardest part because it means getting out there and actually doing something. Thinking about what needs to be done is the easy part, like saying that you are committed to doing it, but doing means facing the unknown and putting your plan into action and this stage is very often where most people fail, because fear prevents us from moving forward.

Continue with it ...

When you commit yourself to making your dream or goal come true, you must have perseverance and be willing to change your approach until you finally reach your desired goal. Depending on what you propose to do this may take some time, but it is essential that you remain as committed to the realization of the project as when you started, it can help to keep a journal of your project from beginning to end, so you can see how far you have come and keep your mind focused on the result you want to achieve. Life has many unexpected peculiarities and can throw anything at us, so it is important that you continue to push yourself through any unexpected difficult moments continuously towards your goal. Once again fear is the main problem and the biggest reason why most people don't achieve and give up what they set out to do, if you give in to fear it will only continue to put bigger obstacles in your way until It finally overcomes you and you give up. The sky is really your limit if you try with perseverance and determination to overcome anything that gets in your way.

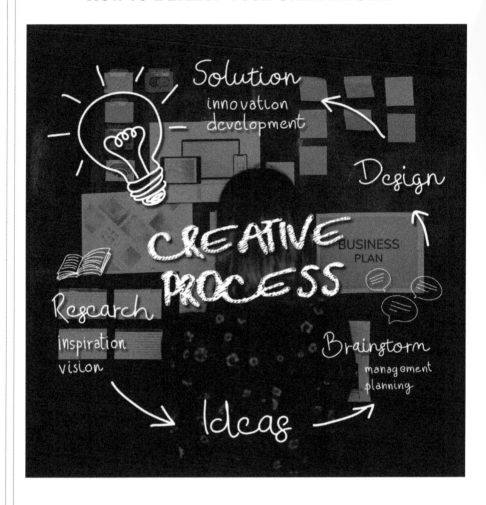

Everyone has a creative side even though sometimes it hides and doesn't surface as quickly as others, but you can develop your creativity by digging deep and practicing, looking for your creative side and bringing it to the forefront. Here are some tips to help you bring out your creative side and expand your creativity.

Create lists

You can expand your creativity enormously and make that side work by making a list every time you have a problem that needs some creative thinking, list as many ideas as you can for solutions and let your creativity flow.

Making changes in your life

Sometimes we can have a creative blockage if we are stuck in a routine, make some changes in your daily life to get the channels flowing again.

Work on the bad ideas

Even if you only come up with bad ideas, you're still creative, so work on the bad ideas and develop them, which, to say it's a bad idea anyway, could become a great idea and the solution to your problems.

Working in a big –

Working in a group and brainstorming together is a great way to develop creativity.

Challenge yourself and others

If you challenge yourself by telling yourself that you can't do something the way you always have, you will have to think of new ways to

Skip

Get around the problem that may lead to some very creative suggestions.

Scribbling

If you are stuck looking for ideas for a solution, then keep a pencil and paper handy and let your imagination run wild and scribble ideas on the paper, it is amazing what will come to mind if you free your mind in this way.

Stimulate the thinking side of your brain

The right side of your brain is where creativity begins, so give it a jolt and wake it up by activating it using the left side, try to breathe using only the left nostril a few times.

Hire a life coach

If you feel that your creativity is really depleted, then consider hiring a life coach to help you find it. A life coach can help you establish the areas where your creativity is lacking and work with you to strengthen it.

Think like a child

Leave behind all your adult obligations, tensions and worries and go back to your childhood, children have the best imagination and their creativity knows no limits, think like a child when you are stuck by creative ideas and soon they will flow freely again.

Relax

Creativity can often run out if we are under great stress, learning a relaxation technique not only makes you feel better but can help clear your mind, give you a fresh start and get your creative side flowing again.

Use some mind games

Have some mind games like logic puzzles at hand, by taking your mind off your problem and solving a puzzle you are using your brain and the use of your brain leads to positive and creative thinking.

Tips and Resources for Creativity

EVERYONE CAN BENEFIT from creativity in their lives. You can use creativity to help with work projects, goal setting, home and family management and much more. To help with all your home and work projects, here are 10 tips to enhance your creativity.

Stay healthy

Find an exercise routine you like and stick to it. Change it whenever you want, but keep doing some kind of exercise. Sleep well. Eat a variety of healthy foods. Meditation or something you like to do to relax can help keep your mind focused.

—

Explore new things

We do so many things without thinking about them. These things become our daily routine, the mundane and boring. Try something new. It can be something as small as taking a different route to work or something like taking a new class on something you've always wanted to learn.

Start thinking like the curious George

Ask yourself about everything you see, hear and read. Why? How? What if... Find out the answers to your questions. You can also keep a curious diary and keep track of all your findings.

Read a new book

Choose one you would not normally choose. Pick one up at the library. If you have always preferred to read non-fiction, pick up a book of fiction. There are so many interesting books to read and so many different genres to choose from. Your librarian will be happy to help you explore new books.

Act like a child

Children are so carefree, honest and fun. Think about what you used to do for fun when you were a kid. Paint a picture, take out those charcoals, finger-paint, go to your local amusement park... everything a child would do! And have fun!

Everyone needs a little time for "me"

Take time every day to relax. You can use meditation if you like to meditate. Don't make plans, don't pay any bills... nothing. Don't do anything for a while.

What if?

What if the end of the world was tomorrow? What if you went to college for business? What if aliens were real? What if there is an afterlife? Make up your own questions and see where your brain takes you.

Never assume anything

Assuming anything always gets someone in trouble. You might assume that your boss is an idiot. What if he doesn't like his life and takes it out on his employees? You might assume that the person who cut you this morning was inconsiderate. What if they were taking your child to the hospital?

Write about yourself

Who are you? What kind of person are you? Where have you been in your life? When are the most important things in your life? Why do you do things the way you do? How do you live your life every day?

Have conversations with people

Listen carefully to what they have to say instead of waiting your turn to speak. What should this person be like? Imagine how they live and think.

LISTEN TO YOUR INNER THOUGHT

We all have feelings about the things that happen in life, they can be discouraging thoughts and feelings or they can be positive, an easy example to listen to your inner thoughts is trying on a dress for a special night. You put on the dress and look in the mirror, automatically think wow, I look great or shake your head and choose another outfit. This is the simplest way to listen to your inner thoughts or intuition when it comes to making the best decision.

However, we can put our inner thoughts to many good uses in our daily lives if we open up and tune in to them. Our inner thoughts can help us to succeed in life, to have more confidence and to live a happier, more productive and satisfying life.

You are the most valuable resource you have in life when it comes to making the right decisions and the right choices. You automatically know if something is right or wrong and how to achieve the best results simply by following your own intuition, and it rarely lets us down.

Channeling into your intuition is easy and here are some simple ways to get started:

- Start with the easiest way to develop your intuition by using it to make less important decisions, for example, choosing what you want for dinner or what movie or restaurant to go to.

- You'll find it easier to tune in to yourself and your inner thoughts when you're calm, so choose a room where you know you won't be disturbed when making important decisions and choices. A good technique to use is to close your eyes and take a couple of deep breaths, concentrate fully on the question or task at hand and see what immediately comes to mind.

- Be willing to admit that you may make mistakes by listening to your intuition, although your intuition is usually correct, you may misinterpret your inner thoughts that may lead to a mistake. However, you must learn from the

---

mistakes you make and continue to develop and strengthen your inner guidance.

- When you let your inner guidance come through, don't confuse things by trying too hard or influencing the response one way or another, chances are that if you are leaning in one direction, then you already have the answer.

Following the above is the easiest way to get your inner guidance to start appearing when you need it, the more you are guided by it and use it, the easier it will be. As the cartoon character "Jiminy cricket" sang to his friend Pinocchio "always let your conscience be your guide", the same applies in real life, follow your heart, your inner thoughts and feelings and you will never go far wrong. It is only when we begin to lose faith and doubt ourselves that we become inattentive and indecisive and this leads us in the wrong direction or to a standstill.

MENTAL IMAGES WORK

One of the most powerful and inspiring tools that can be used daily is something that each of us possesses our own imagination. Your own thoughts, ideas and intuition can be used in your daily life to make positive changes to improve any aspect of your life. Everyone has an imagination, although some of us have a more vivid one that comes to life more quickly than others, but with a little practice, we can all form images in our minds to benefit ourselves.

Using Imagination as a tool

The way you use your imagination to benefit in your daily life is only limited by you, you can use your imagination to visualize any amount of things and use it for almost any situation. Visualization works by forming a positive image of the outcome of a situation and seeing this positive outcome in your mind as if it were happening and letting it replace any negative thoughts you may have had. You should develop visualization as much as you can and look at it from all angles and perspectives, the mental picture you build in your mind should be as clear as possible about how you want the situation to turn out. Think of your imagination and the mental image you build as a blueprint to develop and build upon, just as an architect uses a blueprint when designing a project from start to finish.

The foundations

Start by establishing the foundation of your idea or what you want to change in your mind and slowly build from the bottom up, clearly visualizing every little corner of the idea, the foundation work behind your idea is the basis of your success. As you lay the foundation, think about the following:

• What exactly do I want to achieve or change?

• What difference will this make?

• Can I achieve what I want on my own?

• What do I have to change in my life to achieve this?

• What do I have to learn to do this?

Once you have laid the foundation for whatever you want to change in your life, then you can go ahead and build on your plan, visualize the project every step of the way as clearly as possible and see the project from beginning to end build in your mind as precisely as possible. When you have the visualization completed in your mind then you can take steps to achieve what you want, if you wish you can then write down the steps you took in your mind in writing to achieve the result, and follow them from start to finish.

The key points

The key points to successfully using mental imagery in any aspect of your life are

• Focus the imagination on an idea

• Forming a clear mental image of the idea and the result in your mind.

• Building the idea from foundation to completion

• Successfully executing your plan

TAKING CARE OF YOUR MENTAL HEALTH

To live a happier and healthier life, not only must we take care of our physical health with diet and exercise, but also our mental health.

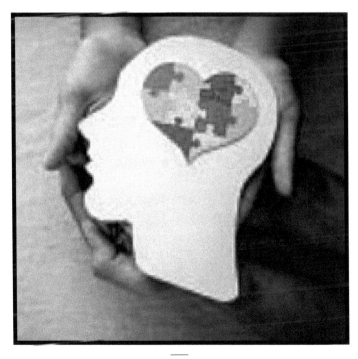

Only by having a complete system of healthy living can you be a healthy person, while exercise is important for your body, it is also important for your mind.

Stress comes to all of us in one form or another with concerns about finances, job security, responsibilities and relationships, all of which affect our mental health. Stress is one of the biggest factors disrupting our mental health and ultimately our well-being. It is just as important to reduce stress in your life as it is to reduce your intake of fat, sugar and calories in order to stay healthy.

There are many ways to take care of our mental health and eliminate some of the stress from our day, some of the steps you can take to stay stress-free include:

- Learn to better manage your day and your time by setting realistic goals that you can meet every day.

- Learn how to use your time more efficiently throughout the day by focusing and completing one task at a time before moving on to another.

- Remain flexible in your thinking when it comes to completing tasks; if you cannot carry them out in the way you had planned, then do it differently.

- Take short breaks throughout the day, this will give you time to clear your head and get back on track and stay focused on the task at hand.

- Admit that you are only human and that you can't do everything, admit when you need a little help and don't be afraid to ask for that help if you need it.

- Learn when to say "no", although we all like to do favors, sometimes we can take too much to our plates and when this happens we can't manage to fit everything in and the stress sets in

- Never try to over-stress your body, you can only do so much in one day, if you try to continually push yourself beyond your limits you will stress your body and mind.

- Learn to recognize when you start to get stressed and take immediate action to relieve that stress

- Learn techniques that allow you to quickly eliminate stress, there is a wide range of techniques you can use, some work better than others and give you better results. Techniques such as breathing exercises and visualization are very effective measures that can be used to quickly relieve stress and allow you to refocus

- Positive affirmations can help deal with stress effectively; a positive mind with positive thoughts is a healthier mind and one for less stress.

- Always make time for a quiet moment, time to relax and do something you like and don't feel guilty about taking this time.

Chapter 3

DAILY HABIT MAKEOVER

DISPELLING FEARS FOR A MORE POSITIVE OUTLOOK

FEARS AND PHOBIAS ARE something that can affect anyone to some extent, while most of us can conquer our fears and most fears and phobias are dislikes rather than real phobias, for some people fear and phobia can be severely distressing and have a great impact on their daily life.

Fears and phobias obviously cause negativity and constant negativity depresses us, while some phobias and fears can be deeply rooted, you can break the control it has over you with time and help. There are several methods of help, and the more deeply rooted the fear or phobia, the more likely it is that professional help in the form of therapy or hypnotherapy will be advised. If the fear is only mild, then you can overcome it by using self-help methods.

Understanding fears and phobias

In order to conquer fears and phobias it is essential that you understand them, fear and phobia simply cause us to think and feel uncomfortable when placed in certain situations. It can bring about feelings such as nausea, vomiting, dizziness, a terrible feeling, a tight band of pressure around the head, chest pains, a feeling of shortness of breath and shaking. These are all feelings that we ourselves allow to build up and take over our mind and body, dispelling the fear is a matter of regaining control and putting things in perspective.

This is the basis for curing any form of fear or phobia although if you suffered for many years it will take longer to recover, recovery is possible. Phobias and fears are basically exaggerated anxiety, and learning methods and ways to relax is a good start to curing fears and phobias. There are many self-help books, DVDs, courses and audio courses that can help you get started, any self-help material designed to address anxiety and stress will help, but there are many aimed specifically at those who suffer from fear and phobia.

The benefits of overcoming fear

The benefit of treating and overcoming phobia and fear are immense and those who have recovered and overcome their fears and phobias have compared it to being reborn again, the world takes on new meaning when fears are dispelled. A new positive perspective is developed that leads to living a happier and more fulfilling life, you start to feel good about yourself and what you can achieve in life, you are finally free to do anything and everything your heart desires.

While there may still occasionally be some anxiety for a while when faced with your fear or phobia, it will be different from the intense fear that once incapacitated you from it. Once you have realized that the key to overcoming these feelings is within you, the fear you feel does not have the same grip it once had and will eventually stop altogether.

OVERCOMING DISSOCIATION

Dissociation causes us problems with our emotions, physical sensations and with what we feel about ourselves and the world around us. It is often associated with depression and anxiety or when a person has gone through a traumatic experience. People who suffer from dissociation have feelings of unreality and often fear that they are going crazy or have some incurable disease. Talking to others and being around them becomes almost impossible and the deep anxiety caused by the feelings can become a social phobia.

The feeling of dissociation can vary from person to person depending on the circumstances that caused it, but common thoughts and feelings associated with dissociation include

- The world around us feels unreal

- Not belonging to the world

- A gray mist that covers your vision

- Like having a veil over your head

- The world is moving at a faster than normal pace

- Confusion

- A terrible feeling of not being able to cope

- You are not sure of yourself

- Others find happiness, but not you.

- Extreme Anxiety

- Feelings that everyone is against you

- Feelings that everyone is talking about you

These are just some of the feelings caused by dissociation and these feelings eventually make the sick person believe that they have to go deeper inside to come back to reality. They continually observe themselves by any brief glimpse of that reality as they know it is returning, of course, the more they turn inward and worry, the worse the symptoms will be.

Cognitive-behavioral therapy can help sufferers overcome feelings of dissociation, especially when severe trauma is the cause. Those who suffer from dissociation due to anxiety and stress may be able to get rid of the feelings through self-help methods and the help and understanding of a physician.

It is important to remember that the world has not really changed, it is only your perception of the world and those around you that have really changed and these are only temporary thoughts and feelings that you are having. Once you have conquered and overcome what is causing the feelings of dissociation you will see things as they were before. For those who suffer from feelings of dissociation due to depression and anxiety they must realize that feelings are just that, no more than feelings and these feelings will go away in time. It is important not to be constantly studying them and wondering when they will go away, to try to accept that they are here for a while and not to dwell on them any longer. Once you've lost interest in your feelings and don't constantly worry about them, it can be surprising how quickly the world turns back into the world you once knew. Accepting your feelings and any thoughts you may have during this period is essential, as only when you lose your fear of the situation can you recover.

OVERCOMING THE DOUBT

Overcoming the doubt is easy, if you don't doubt it, of course. However, most of us harbor an element of doubt in our minds about success when we try something new. In fact, almost everyone is somehow plagued by some kind of doubt. Take science, for example. Do you think that all the scientific progress made would have been possible without questioning the assumptions that prevailed at first? Suppose you want to start a business or launch a new project. Are you absolutely sure you will succeed? There is always a little fear or doubt at first.

Despite your doubt, you cannot let it take you away from your ultimate goal. The reason is simple. You must be prepared to risk failure because it is important to overcome doubt. Immerse yourself in anything without making rash decisions. Don't worry, you won't dive without the

---

right equipment. You will analyze all the possible consequences of your situation and accept the result, whatever it may be. This is the secret to conquering doubt. Have the courage to fight it and you will surely defeat it.

Belief is the enemy of doubt. Learn to think positively and believe in your ability to succeed. Remember that you will succeed if you think you will and you will fail if you think that too. Your thoughts are self-fulfilling prophecies, so you must stop thinking negatively. In the same way, never pay attention to people who discourage you, who delight in sowing doubt in you and who are really wolves in sheep's clothing. Always be in the company of those whose thoughts and attitudes towards life in general are positive.

When failure strikes

You will probably not be lucky enough to never experience failure in your life. However, you must understand that it is part of life. These are the times when failure fills your mind with doubt and it is difficult to regain the confidence you have built up before in the process. You cannot let go of your commitment, no matter how shaken by the failure. In fact, any setback should only prompt you to double your resolve to make another attempt to reach your goal. For this to happen, train your mind to build your self-control and self-confidence. Each step towards self-confidence helps to get rid of doubt and you will return to your successful paths once again.

Healthy doubt

Remember that a certain amount of doubt can always be helpful in gaining wisdom or achieving progress in life. But when it becomes a cause of your depression and inactivity, or when it presents itself as an insurmountable obstacle in your path to your destination, draw upon your reserves of energy that can harden your mind. You must strengthen your will to succeed at all costs and weaken your doubt by all possible means, so that you may lead a full life.

You can succeed because of your doubt or in spite of your doubt. Or, you may have to accept the inevitable and commit to the worst-case scenario. If this happens, change course, re-energize your cylinders and start back on your revised path. Defeat the doubt before it defeats you.

OVERCOMING FEELINGS OF HELPLESSNESS

We all encounter feelings of helplessness to some degree or another at some point in our lives, this is fine as long as we get back on track and overcome these feelings. However, for some, feelings of helplessness settle in and begin to affect our thinking and living. Here are some helpful tips to help you understand these feelings of helplessness and how to overcome them.

Start by identifying the problems, fears, issues and obstacles that make you feel powerless and try to discover why they make you feel that way.

Work in ways that encourage you to assume new beliefs that you can be independent, confident and able to deal with anything that comes up in the future:

- Learn to deal with these feelings of helplessness when they arise

- Practice ways to deal with conflicts and solve problems when they occur

- If you have a relapse and start to doubt again remember that this is normal and pick up where you left off.

- Whatever the success, however small, be sure to reward yourself...

- Realize that it will take time to change our feelings of helplessness, so always strive to achieve your goals.

- Don't aim for perfection all the time, no one is perfect, we all make mistakes.

- Identify what you need to do to grow in self-healing skills and self-confidence.

Feelings of powerlessness can cause us many problems in life, the longer you feel powerless, the less control you will have over your own life; here are some common experiences that occur through powerlessness.

- You begin to feel that no matter what you do or how hard you try, you cannot succeed in life.

- You become too dependent on others around you to help you overcome your problems.

- You see yourself as totally incompetent

- Develops a deep fear that he cannot handle a situation

- You become miserable, unhappy in life and depression sets in

- You consider yourself a victim who always needs to be rescued from situations

- You have a pessimistic view of life in general

- You are afraid that others will see you as a fragile and weak being.

- You get discouraged because you run out of people who are willing to take care of you by solving your problems.

- You resign yourself to the fact that you will always be helpless, that you cannot change...

There are many ways to help you overcome these feelings; the important thing is to remember that you are not alone and that you can take back control of your life and make important decisions to successfully solve your problems. All you need is to have faith in yourself and dig deep and find that faith and bring it to the surface. Although we all have the ability to overcome our problems on our own, it doesn't hurt to get advice from friends and relatives as long as you don't totally trust them to solve your problems for you.

OVERCOMING INTERNAL CONFLICTS

Commitment Makes Life much easier to manage, by making a decision and sticking to it no matter what, and staying committed without letting unwanted thoughts wander through your mind you are able to deal with any obstacle in your path. Internal conflicts lead us nowhere but to indecision and are an open invitation to stress and loss of self confidence.

Although we all have them at some point, it is important that we know how to deal with them and resolve them and move forward again with a positive attitude. By resolving internal conflicts you can greatly improve your self-esteem, allow yourself to be more focused and feel less stressed, listen to your inner voice and guide yourself in making decisions and choices, have total control over your life, manage and achieve the goals you have set for yourself in life and create a healthier, more relaxed and happier future.

Internal conflicts wreak havoc on our emotions and lead to low self-esteem, low self-confidence and depression. With this in mind, it is essential to banish internal conflicts when they arise and not let them start taking over. Internal conflicts can develop in different ways, they can derive from indecision or deep-seated feelings that stem from unresolved issues in your life, they can even derive from things that happened in your childhood. After all, the person you are now is the result of what has happened throughout your life, instead of dealing with the unresolved issues, perhaps you built a wall and kept them inside instead of facing them and dealing with them. It is essential that you break down the wall and bring this out into the open and deal with it now, which is what overcoming unresolved issues and inner conflicts is all about:

- Letting go of the past and the beliefs of the past, including letting go of old habits and emotions, discovering the true inside and listening to the inside.

- Realize that you are able to help yourself and become the person you really are

- Learning to be focused and self-centered, realizing what stresses you out and why

- Making you let go of the feelings and thoughts you harbor related to issues of the past

- Visualize the new you, the more confident and decisive you until it becomes a reality

There are many courses, self-help books, DVDs and audio CDs that can help you overcome the unresolved problems of the past and thus overcome and deal with internal conflicts. However, there is no magic cure and it will take time to resolve these issues and begin to see a better way to deal with and cope with life. While some of us change simply by using self-help methods, others gain more benefit from attending group meetings to see a therapist in the early stages. However, it is important to realize that change is possible and that only you can do it, whatever method you choose to achieve it. It all comes down to basically the same thing, changing your feelings and thoughts.

OVERCOMING BULLYING

BULLYING CAN HAPPEN everywhere, in all walks of life, and can occur in any age group. Being bullied by someone is a form of bullying, it happens at school, in the workplace by peers or the boss, when shopping, and in many other situations.

Some people are not even aware that they are being bullied, while for others it can make their life a misery day after day with them being bullied on a regular basis. It may even be you who is bullying others.

People who are constantly being bullied go through many feelings, but there are many steps that can be taken to help eliminate bullying. In order to successfully deal with bullying, you must first understand what bullying really is, it can come in many guises.

• Use force to get what you want from others

- Threatening or using power and control to get others to do what you want

- Make others think they are more powerful than you

- Using size or force to make others do what you want or threaten them

- Keeping the punishments over your head, such as being fired, whipped or divorced.

- Being bad-tempered, angry or upset with someone for doing what you want.

- Behave in such a way that others are afraid to approach you...

- Use your wealth to get others to do what you want

- Use of racial or sexual insults towards others

There are many steps you can take to stop allowing others to intimidate you, the first step is to look at yourself and determine if your irrational and unhealthy thinking has allowed you to be intimidated by others. If you think this might have been the case, then you should take steps to

- Identify new, healthier ways of thinking to help you overcome and respond to bullying

- Show your new ways of thinking and acting to those who are bullying you, this will show them that you are no longer willing to be bullied by them

- Develop ways of dealing with people in case they respond negatively to the new you

- See the consequences of your new assertive behavior

- Stick to your guns and accept the consequences of your new behavior...

The next step to take once you have developed a strategy for dealing with those who bully you is to develop ways to reinforce your beliefs in the new you. The easiest way is to use daily affirmations or positive self-dialogue. Examples of positive self-dialogue include

- I am a good person, who is dignified and deserves to be treated with respect.

- I will not put anyone in a superhuman position over me

- I will regain control of my life from anyone who tries to intimidate me in the future.

- I will not allow others to intimidate me

- There is no one out there who can intimidate me

OVERCOMING THE NEED TO BE IN CONTROL

Some of us have trouble being in control, we simply have the urge to control all aspects of the lives of those around us and this can lead to many problems. There are many negative effects that come with the compulsive need to fix everyone's problems and they can have a severe effect on your life in general. So what is the need to be in control or to fix? Also, what are the negative effects, and how can you help yourself give up the need to be in control?

You could say that you have a problem with needing to be in control if any of the following points apply to you or someone you know.

- You compulsively go to the rescue of someone, regardless of whether they ask for help or not, just because you believe that is the way the task or situation should be treated.

- The feeling that other people are in need becomes an automatic response for you.

- You firmly believe that things have to be perfect or right for people, otherwise they cannot be happy in life.

- You feel you have to change people because you can't accept them as they are.

- You firmly believe that you know what is best for others and you strive to get them to see things your way.

- You accept personal responsibility for the actions of others.

- You can't help but give advice to others or offer your help.

- People see you as an interference in their lives.

- You have a strong need to feel wanted or needed, which leads you to become too involved in the affairs of others.

- Things don't feel right if you're not helping others or fixing their problems.

- The most common negative effects that compulsive behavior like this can have on a person include

- Develops relationships where people become too dependent on you

- You cannot remain emotionally uninvolved if you meet someone you see who needs your help.

- You lose friendships because you need to be in control of their lives.

- You begin to neglect your own needs in favor of dealing with others around you.

- You feel guilty if things don't get better for a person.

- You may be angry with those you have helped if they do not show enough recognition for what you have done.

- Develops low self-esteem by getting lost with others.

- Ways you can develop to overcome the need for control are

- To have the belief that others have the ability to fix their own problems.

- Set a boundary between those who you think need your help.

- Don't get hooked on needing recognition from others.

- Accept that the only person you should control is yourself.

- Tell people to confront you if you try to give them unwanted help or advice.

- Realize that people have the ability to change themselves if they want to.

- It only offers help to those who clearly ask for it.

OVERCOMING THE TRAUMA

There are many thoughts and feelings associated with a traumatic experience, trauma occurs when we are faced with any terrible situation, such as a car accident, a fire, witnessing an accident, a natural disaster, an attack on you, war, etc. Many people who are recovering from a traumatic experience mentally block out the experience that caused the distress while others relive it over and over again.

Trauma can bring up many feelings like:

Shock

Shock is a normal reaction to any traumatic experience and the closer you are to the experience, the more shock occurs. Your brain has to process the terrible images you have seen and that is when the sensation of shock sets in and takes time to digest.

Disbelief

Many people who experience a shocking situation have a strong belief that what they have witnessed may not have happened.

Denial

Many people deny that the event occurred; they try to force it out of their minds.

Emotional pain

Even if you have not been hurt in the incident, you will feel the pain of those around you who did.

Anger

After the shock, the anger will set in, you will wonder "why did this happen to you" and you will be able to feel anger towards anyone and everyone.

Guilt

Very often we blame ourselves or others for what has happened, we can even blame God for letting this happen.

Sadness

As you overcome a particular traumatic experience, you will feel waves of sadness that will suddenly overwhelm you.

Depression

For some time after the experience you may fall into a depression from time to time.

Anxiety

Anxiety often develops from fear and may continue for some time after the experience.

All of the above are the most common feelings and thoughts associated with having gone through a trauma; these feelings can come in no particular order and at any time. What you should realize is that these feelings are natural and are the way your body and mind deal with what has happened; the feelings and thoughts will dissipate over time.

There are many ways to deal with them and help yourself overcome them, the best way for you, of course, will depend on the severity of the trauma you have been exposed to. However, there are a number of coping skills that can be learned to help you overcome the trauma.

- Taking what happened and letting it all out;

- Listening and accepting advice from family, friends or the counselor;

- Accepting what happened and moving on with life;

- Change your environment;

- Participate in recreational activities;

- Picking up your old daily routine;

- Participation in seminars.

Chapter 4

FREEDOM FORGE

DEVELOPING YOUR SELF-IMAGE

HOW YOU SEE YOURSELF goes far beyond how you feel about yourself and how others see and think about you. If you think positively on the inside, then you will shine with confidence on the outside and you will find yourself in this way with others. Feeling good about yourself is essential if you want to be happy in life and get the most out of it, it can make the difference between succeeding and failing, it all depends on how you see the image you have of yourself.

People suffer from low self-esteem for many reasons and if they have been raised feeling negatively about themselves, developing a positive self-image will be difficult, but not impossible. Developing a positive image is about changing the thoughts and feelings about yourself and if you have had negative thoughts for a long time, changing the habit will take time. However, by adapting a new way of thinking and adhering to this new way of thinking, you will eventually banish unwanted negative feelings and automatically replace them with positive ones in your daily life. When this happens, your perspective changes and with your perspective, you change, where once you might have thought something would be beyond your capabilities, you will now see it in a different light and begin to realize that it is within your reach.

There are many ways you can use to develop a more positive self-image and self esteem, there are self-help books dedicated to the subject, audio sessions that you listen to and follow, DVDs, hypnotherapy audio or attend counseling sessions. However, they are all based on basically the same principle, understanding what trust really is, gaining confidence in yourself, getting rid of negative beliefs and replacing them with positive ones, and learning strategies that will allow you to remain confident in any situation.

The foundations for developing a more positive perspective and self-image are

- Thinking about a positive self-image and confidence and understanding what it means to you

- Know yourself better, recognize your strengths and build on those strengths

- Constantly advancing and changing negative thoughts into more positive ones

- Reflecting on what you have learned and seeing the positive changes you are making in your life

We all speak to ourselves at one time or another, and we may find ourselves continually belittling ourselves and being too slow to praise ourselves. This must be changed. We want to change the useless talk and replace it with positive and encouraging talk, the easiest way to do this is

- Get rid of irrational thoughts and replace them with rational thoughts

- Replace negative thoughts and feelings with positive ones

- Give yourself credit

- Repeat the positive statements to yourself as needed throughout the day

CHANGE THE SHAPE OF YOUR PERSONAL IMAGE

Although we all Understand the importance of eating healthy, exercising and dieting, very few realize that changing our self-image is just as important to a healthy lifestyle. The way you think and feel about yourself contributes greatly to bringing happiness and success to your life and to change your self-image, just as you give your body a workout, you need to give your mind a workout as well.

The first step you must take is to determine exactly what you would like to be and what you are already good at or enjoy doing. You could say you are good at sports, poetry and spending time with friends. The only thing you don't want to do is create a list of things you don't like about yourself. This would only make you feel inadequate and hinder your ability to change yourself and your self-image. By focusing on the good things about yourself, you will be able to quickly change your self-image into something you can be proud of.

Visualization and affirmations can help you realize how great you already are. Look at yourself doing and becoming everything you originally wrote. Repeat the positive affirmations throughout the day to help the new way of thinking settle in and develop your new positive perspective. By vividly imagining this new you, your mind will retrain itself until you understand that all the things you visualize are true.

Consider keeping a journal

DURING THIS PROCESS you will benefit from keeping a journal about your transformation, you will be able to look back and this will help strengthen your self-image and reinforce the new you. It is important that you leave your past and think only of the future and the new you, you will develop your new self-image more quickly by focusing on what you are achieving and what you have yet to achieve.

The objectives will take you there

YOU CAN HELP SHAPE a positive image of yourself if you set attainable goals for yourself and then strive to achieve them. Giving yourself something to work on creates success in your life - a vital part of reshaping your self-image. Set goals for yourself in whatever area you desire, work, personal, health, fitness and then go for it. Set a realistic time frame for achieving each goal and praise yourself when you achieve it.

How you choose to change your image is entirely up to you, there are no limitations to what you can achieve if you set your mind to it and are determined to work towards the desired goal. If you stray from the path that leads you there, then don't get discouraged, get back on track and move forward with determination.

You commit to working hard to achieve what you want. Plan what you will do when you finally reach your final goal, you must aim to give yourself special treatment, you deserve it. Make sure it's something you can put your mind to during hard times, keeping it in mind will give you an incentive that will be completely worthwhile.

HOW KEEPING A JOURNAL CAN HELP YOU SUCCEED

YOU SHOULD NEVER UNDERESTIMATE the power of keeping a written journal, there are many ways a journal can help you be more successful in life. You can use it to help you associate your feelings with your thoughts and your thoughts with your feelings and this is the most important thing to succeed in life. Your journal can help you find out what motivates you in life, develop new skills, learn new strategies for coping with life in general, write down ideas and plan for them, and find out more about the person you are by asking questions about yourself and writing down the answers to those questions. A journal is an essential tool when it comes to learning about ourselves and if we want to succeed in life, and knowing yourself is a necessity. Although we may think, we know very few of us actually do. By keeping a journal, we begin to realize all the little things we don't really know or understand about ourselves.

Develop your intuition

YOUR OWN INTUITION is your greatest asset and if more people would develop an ear for what we are really saying inside, then more of us would know the way forward and how to successfully achieve what we want from life, simply by following our own inner guidance. Your own personal journal can be a great way to develop your intuition and listen to yourself and what's inside of you, record all the little things you might miss, like flashes of inspiration, premonitions or hunches about something, basically anything your intuition is telling you.

Keeping a journal is essential because inspiration can come at any time, some of the greatest inventors and thinkers kept journals including one of the most prolific inventors in history, Thomas Edison. One of the most useful things that a journal does is to give us the ability to look back at the records and refer to them, for example, if a problem was found and overcome in the past and a similar problem arises, then one can reflect and apply the same solution or adapt it for a more positive outcome. Your journal can remind you of past achievements and this contributes greatly to building self-confidence and helping you succeed in life when things get difficult and can help you feel comfortable.

Learn from the past

One technique that is very popular and can help you keep a journal is the "best" technique. This technique can be applied to any situation that comes up in life and is based on simply looking at the situation and finding out what you liked or what you experienced from it and then deciding how you could do better next time or how you could have experienced better from it. The key to recovering from past mistakes and succeeding in the future is to learn from your mistakes, but remember to focus on your strengths rather than your weaknesses. If you focus more on your weaknesses than on your strengths, very often this leads you to unconsciously reinforce them, which in turn leads to low self-esteem, and of course having low self-esteem is not positive. Only by building on your strengths can you increase your self-esteem and your self-esteem is the crucial factor in understanding your weaknesses and correcting them and therefore building a positive outlook on life that greatly increases your chances of success. So, by writing down your experiences in your journal, you can look back and gain a clearer understanding of yourself and how you feel, which ultimately determines how you think and how you think determines the success you have in life.

Starting early to combat low self-esteem

Health care providers know that there are many reasons why people suffer from low self-esteem, from chemical imbalance to lack of faith, opportunity, discipline and more. However, many agree that the main cause of low self-esteem is due to a lack of positive feedback and love given to children during their early years.

What happens too often is that children are born before their parents have matured enough to focus more clearly on their own adulthood, family and family values, on the race to succeed with a partner while both work long hours, continue to try to learn good work and life ethics and morals while outside the influence of their parents, and learn about family life together and extended family members during those early years. It's a lot to take in all at once.

And often, before mature adults realize they may be following in their own parents' footsteps, they repeat the same mistakes they made in their own childhood. For example, many parents simply don't let their children try again and again and make their own mistakes. And many parents don't offer their children sincere praise and compliments, but take them and their efforts for granted in a difficult, harsh, and challenging world.

Another important factor is that children often truly believe in their hearts that all adults are right, and establish their own values and feedback systems for them. Unfortunately, however, too many of these adults who raise young children continue to struggle with substance abuse, gambling, alcohol abuse, and other very important issues. The result is that these adults are simply not doing what is best for them or their families, especially with their young children trying to follow in their footsteps. What a drug or alcohol abuser does not see, for example, is the physical, emotional, and often other abuses that are passed on to children as adults become too caught up in their own approach.

In short, children and adults of all ages need a positive response and a sincere demonstration of care and concern. Start young and encourage your partner and children to make good, healthy and positive choices. And when they fail at something, offer them hope and encouragement to try again.

It also encourages education, no matter what level you have. Too many adults tend to "say" that they want their children to succeed, but deny the comments throughout childhood in the areas of educational advancement. So, offer lots of reading materials at home, set an example and read yourself, encourage workshops, online classes, e-books, and more. Try to point out and help guide children and their peers in the areas where they are strongest, such as school subjects (chess, math, music...), hobbies (crafts, musical instruments, singing...), and service to others (volunteer work, part-time work).

He holds out his hand and shows a positive reaction. And arrive with human love, care and respect. You will gain in return, increasing your own self-esteem and love.

STOP UNDERESTIMATING YOUR VALUE

IT IS IMPORTANT THAT you do not underestimate your value, because you are what you think you are, self-esteem is about thoughts and what you think of yourself. If you think about confidence, then you will seem confident, and this will show on the outside, when people realize their value, they will be able to face life with more confidence and optimism about the future. They are more likely to be able to achieve their goals and gain experience, satisfaction and happiness from life, are more capable of forming lasting relationships that work, and are better able to cope with whatever life throws at them. A person who realizes his or her self-esteem is a happy and well-adjusted person who possesses the ability to cope with anything and anyone throughout his or her life and is capable of doing anything he or she sets out to do.

Problems caused by underestimating your self-esteem

MANY PROBLEMS CAN OCCUR in your life simply by underestimating your own self-esteem, lack of self-esteem affects your sense of well-being, causes problems with your feelings and needs, affects your ability to make good healthy decisions in relationships, work and life in general and causes fears such as abandonment and problems such as people who continually strive for perfection but never seem to reach it. Lack of self-esteem has been attributed to indecision, addictions such as smoking, drinking, drug abuse, compulsive shopping disorder, and eating problems such as bulimia and anorexia.

Realizing your self-esteem

EACH OF US IS CAPABLE of realizing our self-esteem, we don't have to do anything special to gain or deserve self-esteem. The key to realizing your self-esteem is to get that little voice inside your head to stop belittling it all the time, it is our own thoughts and feelings that drive us to develop low self-esteem. This little voice has developed over a long period of time, casting doubt on ourselves until we genuinely believe that

---

we are not worthy or capable, it is our own minds that develop our feelings of low self-esteem, not some external force. There are several ways you can begin to change your thinking pattern and increase your self-esteem which in turn begins the process of realizing your true self-worth, the foundations behind making this correction are

- Learn to recognize self-critical thoughts and stop them

- Learn to substitute your own thoughts for more positive ones

- Keeping the habit of correcting your negative thoughts with more positive ones

There are many ways to begin to establish the pattern of changed thoughts, but perhaps the easiest is to use affirmations, which are simple positive statements and use them to replace any negative thoughts, examples of positive affirmations might be

- This is a new and exciting challenge - this could be used to replace thoughts like this is very difficult or I can't do this is beyond me.

- I am a safe and dignified individual... replace this when you have thoughts like "I can do this or I could never do this".

- I can do anything my heat desires if I put my mind to it - this can be used to replace thoughts as I am not sure I am capable of completing

---

81

this task or I do not know if I can complete what is asked of me.

These are all simple statements that you can use to gradually change the way you think, that will eventually change the way you feel about yourself and encourage you to realize your true self-worth.

DEVELOPING YOUR FULL POTENTIAL

While many of us are happy in life and achieve to some extent what we set out to do, there are not many who actually push themselves a little further and develop their full potential. While we may be particularly good at doing certain things in life, we could excel if we had the courage and faith in ourselves to do so.

As children we are full of great ideas, they never stop flowing because we have an open mind and the belief in ourselves that we can achieve almost anything. However, as we grow up, the fear of doing the right thing and talking and being ridiculed takes over and slows the flow of our imagination and ideas. We hold back our thoughts and this can prevent us from realizing our full potential.

There are many ways to start developing your potential, it's never too late. You must remember that there is no right or wrong way to think and many times the reason others try to make you feel inferior when you express opinions and ideas is because they wish they had the idea and the

—

courage to speak out. So concentrate on your skills and abilities and let your thoughts run free, put them into practice and really excel in life.

To succeed you must realize that sometimes you will make mistakes, no one is perfect and mistakes are fine as long as you recognize them and learn from them. Features that you can cultivate that will lead you to develop your true and full potential include

Working hard

Putting all of you into everything you do when you work towards what you want in life

Be patient,

Things don't happen overnight, so be patient and you will be rewarded.

Determination

Stick to your guns and never give in when things don't go your way or you run into obstacles

Commitment

Commit to your goals and what you need to achieve, set goals in mind and don't let anything or anyone stand in your way of achieving them

Organizational skills

The more organized you are the easier the path to success, plan your ideas to the max before putting them into action

Learn from mistakes

You will make mistakes along the way but you can learn valuable lessons from them and move on

Self-confidence

You have to have confidence in yourself and believe in yourself and your ideas, there is no room for doubt

Be realistic

Don't set goals that you can't realistically achieve in a given time, by setting unrealistic goals you are exposing yourself to failure over and over again.

When you develop your full potential, the two most important things to remember are what you want from life and what you can realistically do to make it happen. Once you have these facts clear, then you can go full steam ahead towards achieving what you want.

Starting Slowly Gives Great Rewards

Even if you can't to the mailbox without huffing and puffing, you can run to boost your self-esteem. The first time you run to the mailbox, down the street, around the block or any distance, you will feel a great sense of pride and accomplishment. The first time you go out, you'll probably do a lot more walking than running. However, if you keep this up, you will soon find yourself running more and more until one day you run the entire route without stopping.

The important thing to remember is to start slowly and not overdo it at first. Your body needs to adjust to your new levels of activity, especially if you previously lead a sedentary lifestyle. Exaggerating and causing overuse injuries can be a great discouragement, especially after seeing the progress you have made. Most people won't want to increase their weekly mileage by more than 10%. However, do what is best for you - some people can handle a larger increase in mileage and others need to increase mileage much more slowly.

Running is 90% mental

Despite how the muscles feel, 90% of the races are purely about the mental capacity to do so. Building this side of your brain by telling yourself that you can do it, that you can finish the race, that you can run for 30 minutes without stopping, or whatever your goal is will invariably be a sure way to build your self-esteem. What happens is that while you are running, in order to finish, you will have to make up some good things to say to yourself, which is often referred to as positive self-satisfaction. Not only does this talk help you get through your current race, but it will seep into the rest of your life and you'll find yourself using it at work, while doing the dishes and heavy lifting won't make you feel so bad anymore.

Goal setting...

With a Career, you can set goals big and small. For the beginning runner, a good goal might be to complete a local 5k. You'll certainly enjoy the

---

feeling of accomplishment, not to mention the right to show off at the office.

Remember to set realistic running goals and you will increase your self-esteem, and the miles, much faster.

HOW TO UNEARTH YOUR HIDDEN FORCES

Have you even realized that you, like anyone else, have a gold mine of strength at the bottom of your heart? Most of us are not aware of the fact that we possess such hidden talents. The rest of us, although we know they are there within us, do not know how to bring the forces out into the open and use them to improve the quality of our lives or to lead a more fulfilling life. Let's explore ways and means of unearthing our hidden strengths to enrich our lives.

To begin with, you must believe that you have some inherent strengths. Banish all negativity in thought and action. Never say to yourself, "I can't." I don't have it in me. Instead, think that you have the strength within you to deal with any situation, no matter what it is, and that you can, and certainly will, succeed in dealing with it in an appropriate manner. Remember, self-confidence is confidence and gaining confidence is half the battle.

The next step is to start exploring your own being.

Closely examine your background, both genetic and acquired. Not that you haven't done this before. It's quite possible that you have. Now you need to do it more systematically. Write down what you inherited from your parents or grandparents. If you think you haven't inherited anything, think about what you have been taught. Is it possible that somewhere deep inside you, you have those same strengths, but you haven't realized that you could use them? Make a list of all your parents' or grandparents' strengths and talents. See if some or all of them can be used. For example, does music run in the family? Did you ever notice that your mother was very patient? You can have it in you too, without being aware of it. Have you ever noticed that you have, by nature, a skill with words that others you know do not have? Have you not put this skill to good use? You may be gifted with a strong physique, but you are not aware of the ways in which your physical strength can be put to good use. Explore, experiment, and eventually explode. That should be your strategy to bring your strength to light.

Educational strengths

Your acquired background seems easier to analyze. But in reality you need a more detailed examination. Again, make a detailed list of the strengths your education and training have given you. What is the skill set you have acquired? Are you using your skills and talents to their fullest extent? Have you pursued your interests, turned some of them into hobbies, and thought about turning at least one of the latter into a second career? Enlist your inner strengths such as composure, compassion, conflict resolution, self-control, perseverance or determination, etc. to achieve success in your life.

—

This is not a once-in-a-lifetime exercise. As your life continues to progress, periodic reviews of your strengths help you identify unknown strengths that can help you follow the right path. Who knows, you may find gold!

How NLP CAN HELP YOU

Many of those who encounter NLP for the first time are likely to wonder what it is all about, even though it appears in the context of influencing human behavior through the adoption and practice of certain established techniques and procedures. In reality, NLP stands for Neuro-Linguistic Programming, where 'neuro' is something related to both the mind and the body, 'linguistic' refers to the patterns or structures of language, and 'programming' is devising ways and means of coordinating mind, body, and language to shape behavior in ways that achieve better results than before in various areas of life. In a sense, NLP can help you in many ways, if you only get to know its techniques and how to use them for your benefit.

Changes in perceptions

You can turn to NLP when you are interested in developing your personality traits and characteristics, which determine your verbal and non-verbal reactions to events in this world.

As a first step, let's understand that your perception of reality is based on your subjectivity. Just as a map is nothing more than a miniature representation of a territory, what you perceive as real is only a colored representation of reality, not reality itself. You cannot avoid looking at the world through pink glasses. Your reactions are not dictated by reality but by your vision of that reality.

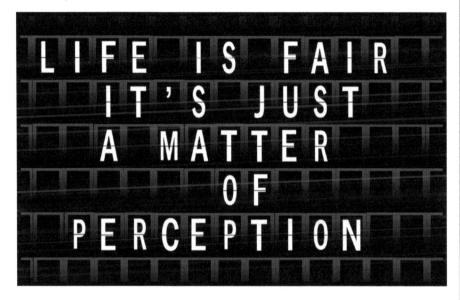

NLP helps you realize this and reduce, if not completely eliminate, your subjectivity. Then you might consider adopting alternative views of reality and consequently bring about a change in the way you react to it.

Why do people react differently to a particular event or situation? Is it not because of differences in their individual perceptions of that event or situation? What a traumatic event is to one may not be the same to another. For example, some people may take verbal or physical abuse lightly or simply ignore it. Others may be so affected by it that they need psychological or medical treatment. The underlying philosophy of NLP is based on the premise that it is possible to change one's perceptions, beliefs and behavior so that traumatic experiences can be treated. It is also possible to become immune to trauma.

Getting rid of phobias

IN THE SAME WAY, YOU can get rid of your phobias, if you have them, by getting into the factors that cause your fear in the first place, with the help of NLP techniques. Maybe you can see things the way your opponents do. Maybe you can consider the same things from a totally new perspective. Or, perhaps you can study people who have achieved excellence in any particular aspect of their life, find out what qualities and factors contributed to their success, and then try to import the same or similar factors and qualities into your life in an effort to achieve excellence in your chosen field. You can reduce your levels of unhappiness or increase your levels of happiness by transforming your portfolio of beliefs, your preconceived notions, your language patterns that show your innermost feelings, your unconscious mind that exposes your conscious reactions to the outside world, and so on. In short, as NLP practitioners claim, NLP transforms you into a new you, a happier you, and a more effective you

---

capable of dealing with this world in a much better way than before.

Clearing the way for success

If we are surrounded by disorder and disorganization in our lives it is an excellent breeding ground for negativity, negativity is what causes feelings of low self-esteem and low self-worth that hinder us in life and is the basis for us not succeeding in what we decide to do. Therefore, if we want to succeed and make the most of life, it is essential that we clear ourselves from time to time and remove any excess of obstacles and belongings from our path, keeping our lives open and free. Here are some simple points to remember to keep your home and life free of clutter.

Replace the old with the new

THIS APPLIES TO ANYTHING you bring into your home, whether it's clothes, utensils, furniture or any other item, if you continually buy and bring new items into your home then very quickly you're going to be overloaded with items that usually end up being packed in cartons and put in the basement. Even if you pack up items and put them in the basement it is still a mess, a mess you could do without, so get into the habit of throwing things away or donating them to charity when you buy new ones.

Don't save unnecessary things

To keep your home free of clutter it is essential that you do not keep anything that is not essential, items that fall into this category include junk mail that appears through your mailbox, flyers, old newspapers, magazines, letters, or junk from your car. Letters that are not needed can be shredded immediately, the same goes for junk mail, while your car's trash should be picked up daily and disposed of immediately. It's amazing if you get used to the amount of trash you can dispose of daily in your home just by being careful with items like this.

Throw away everything you don't like

Never hold on to an object simply because it has been given to you, even though this may seem hard, it leads to unnecessary mess, if you don't like something, don't keep it, give it to someone who likes it or sell it but don't hold on to it.

Have a goal

WHEN LOOKING AROUND your house, have a goal in mind when you clear the room, for example, treat each room separately and say to yourself, "I have a goal of clearing this room by 25%. If you start with a clear goal in mind you will feel more in control, organized and feel like you are accomplishing something. You should divide the clutter into three piles, the items you can sell, the items that are trash and the items you want to donate to charity, starting with a plan and a clear goal in mind makes messing up your life much easier.

Never postpone

Be hard on yourself and don't feel guilty about throwing something away or giving it away, once you start to clear your head don't think twice and take something out of a pile and change your mind about getting rid of the feeling. If we stop to think about each item in this way, we sow the seeds of doubt and negativity that lead to disorganization and a home full of items we don't need.

CONCLUSION

People taught us that everything we see outside that disturbs us is part of us. What if it is not? What if it's just a psychological way of conditioning us in this too?

I firmly believe that we are all made of the same material, we all have the same organs, and many of us look so much alike that we think we are the same person, but we are not!

Thank goodness we are all the same but different in character, soul and spirit!

Each of us has his path, his own time of evolution, some more rapid, some less rapid, each of us has his personal history that has little to do with us. Of course, there may be some similarities, but we are not us. It is always his story with his troubles and his pathologies, and we with ours.

Honestly, I don't want to be a reflection of anyone and the only mirror I want to reflect myself in is the one in my own home. No, I don't put my ego in the way because I'm not looking for perfection or comparison. I want to be free to be what I am as I am, without having to look in someone else's mirror.

I'm convinced that the work we have to do on ourselves is our own. We can look at those who are doing less well and maybe learn something to put into practice on ourselves.

If I see badness around me, it doesn't mean that inside I see badness, but maybe my character, personality, and the soul itself see that attitude, that situation as badness.

We are free to feel what we feel without feeling guilty and pointing the finger at ourselves for whatever others are willing to do, and we are free to be good ugly, nasty, kind, angry in short, we are what we are.

I am not another you; I am me as I am.

All of us together are part of a great truth that maybe one day we will discover, but until then, I prefer to look at myself in the mirror of my house, happy to be just me and my reflection.

ABOUT THE AUTHOR ELDON WELLS

Eldon Wells began his life journey in New Jersey, America. As a young boy, he traveled the world to discover new cultures. Wandering around on his own and meeting many people and challenging himself, he discovered that happiness is actually within ourselves and can be found anywhere as long as we are willing to implement a lifestyle that is free from conditioning and unique.

He is a sportsman and loves hiking and skiing. He likes the mountains.

Characteristically, he is an introspective and balanced person and for this reason he studied psychology and graduated with honors. After that he obtained a master's degree in personal development and started his activity by conducting thematic seminars where his approach has the characteristic of enhancing personal performance to master life and achieve success and happiness.

Eldon is now 46 years old and married to Linda Green, whom he met at a conference in London, and they have a daughter named Anna.

CPSIA information can be obtained
at www.ICGtesting.com
Printed in the USA
LVHW051206160621
690359LV00008B/383

9 781802 933604